PLANET GRETA

CONTENTS

STRIKE ONE

On Monday 20 August 2018, when Greta Thunberg was just 15, she walked out of school and headed to the Swedish parliament. Greta took her bike, some climate change fact sheets and a hand-painted sign that read: 'Skolstrejk för klimatet' ('School strike for the climate'). Her message was simple:

"We know there is a problem, so why is nothing being done? If the grown-ups don't learn their lessons, why should we bother going to ours?"

Greta's parents weren't sure they approved of their daughter missing school, and not one of her classmates joined her, but Greta was determined to make her voice heard.

The teenager went back to protest each day until the Swedish national elections on 9 September. Greta demanded that her government reduce carbon emissions in line with the Paris Agreement, a historic deal that unites all the world's nations in a single agreement on tackling climate change.

Day by day, more protesters joined Greta, including schoolchildren, grandparents and scientists. Her message that urgent action is needed to combat climate change spread across borders and continents.

Now the number of strikers is estimated at 7 million, in over 185 countries worldwide.

THE POWER OF ONE

Greta's schoolgirl strike quickly turned into a full-on movement with no signs of stopping. Soon, Greta and her fellow early strikers founded **Fridays for Future**. Greta announced that she would go back to school, but every Friday she would strike to spread her message. Across the world, other students were inspired to join in the Friday climate strikes. Many of the children involved were under voting age, so for them, this was their way of making their voices heard.

FRIDAYS FOR FUTURE

FIGHTING THE FLAMES

Greta began to speak up. She was not afraid to deliver her powerful message, even if it wasn't something that people wanted to hear. She said:

"Our house is on fire. I am here to say, our house is on fire. Adults keep saying: 'We owe it to the young people to give them hope.' But I don't want your hope. I don't want you to be hopeful. I want you to panic. I want you to feel the fear I feel every day. And then I want you to act."

SCIENCE SPEAKS

Greta is fighting for what she calls **the climate crisis**. She wants everyone to listen to the science, young and old.

The world's temperature is increasing too quickly...

Scientists say that we need to stop the world's temperature from rising any more than 1.5°C.

But worryingly, it looks like the temperature is set to rise by 3°C this century.

We need to ACT FAST. Greta is urging countries to cut their emissions of greenhouse gases and asking individuals to make lifestyle choices that can help our planet.

Greta says:
THE TIME IS NOW.

ALL ABOUT

GRETA

Growing up, Greta was always quiet, shy and clever. Even now, missing every Friday of school and travelling the world, she remains at the top of her class. She says she was the invisible girl at the back who no one saw, and she spoke only when necessary.

Name: Greta Thunberg

Date of birth: 3 January 2003

Hometown: Stockholm, Sweden

Pets: two dogs

Favourite foods: salads, falafels and noodles (all vegan)

Favourite hobbies: cycling, reading, singing and walking her dogs

Famous supporters: Maisie Williams, Jameela Jamil, Ellie Goulding, Barack Obama, Anne Hathaway and Meghan, Duchess of Sussex

GROWING UP

Greta first became worried by changes to the planet's climate as a young girl, aged eight. At school, Greta's class was shown a documentary about plastic pollution in the world's oceans, and the deadly effects it can have on polar bears, seabirds and marine mammals. Greta was left in tears, not only because of the fate of these animals, but because it seemed to Greta that no one was acting to tackle the problem. How could people carry on living their lives – taking flights or making car journeys that polluted the planet, or using plastic that would end up in the ocean?

TAKING ACTION

If no one else was going to act, Greta decided that she would do something on her own. She wrote an article about her concerns for the environment that won a competition in the Swedish newspaper the *Svenska Dagbladet*. Following that, she met with environmentalists to discuss ideas about how to protest.

CHANGES AT HOME

One of Greta's first jobs was to convince her family to make lifestyle changes. She challenged them to reduce their carbon footprint. Her family became mostly vegan and stopped travelling by air – instead using trains and investing in an electric car.

SEEING IN BLACK AND WHITE

Greta has been diagnosed with Asperger syndrome. This means that she sees the world differently to other people. She says it makes her see things in black and white and calls it her **superpower**. She sees the climate crisis as extremely upsetting, which makes her want and need to act.

"It makes me different, and being different is a gift, I would say."

COMING OUT ON TOP

When Greta was 11 years old, she was diagnosed by her doctor with depression. Climate change wasn't the only reason for this depression, but it played a part. Greta was deeply affected by what she had learned about global warming and she became very upset. The condition was so serious that it stopped her from doing everyday things, such as going to school and even eating. Greta lost over 9 kg (20 lb) in just two months. It wasn't until she started talking to her parents about her environmental concerns – and realizing that she could help – that Greta could move on from this dark time. If you or someone you know is upset or worried, don't stay silent. Talk to a trusted adult and ask for their support.

A FORCE FOR CHANGE

Greta began to understand that she could do something positive with her life. She didn't want to waste her time feeling so down about things – instead, she would change them! It was a slow process to heal and gain weight to be healthy again, but Greta was determined. Greta realized that by talking about her worries, she could influence others and make a difference. Once her family started making lifestyle changes, Greta began to think bigger – she wanted to take action and help turn the negatives into positives.

FAMILY LIFE

When she's not protesting and speaking with influencers around the world, Greta lives at home in Stockholm, Sweden, with her mum, dad, sister and two dogs.

Dad: Svante Thunberg

Greta's dad, Svante, is an actor, who also works as manager and producer for Malena. He is involved in his daughter's activist efforts and travelled with her across the Atlantic Ocean by boat in August 2019 so that Greta could attend two important global climate change gatherings.

Mum: Malena Ernman

Greta's mum, Malena, is a famous Swedish opera singer. She has sung at festivals and concerts around the world. In 2016, Malena ended her international performances when Greta convinced her to give up air travel, for the good of the environment.

Sister: Beata Ernman Thunberg

Beata is Greta's younger sister. She is a vegan like Greta and a singer and songwriter like Malena!

FOLLOW GRETA

When Greta first began striking from school, she used social media to share her campaign with others who felt the same way about environmental issues. The word spread to journalists, too, who gave Greta's story coverage in the media. Now Greta has over 7 million followers on Instagram and more than 2 million fans on Facebook, who can help spread her message across the world.

Although support for Greta and her mission has exploded online, many have criticized her and her work, including some people who claim that global warming doesn't exist. Greta, though, chooses to ignore the haters – she is determined that nothing will stop her presenting the facts about climate change.

If you're old enough to go online, you can follow Greta's work or contact her via the following platforms:

@gretathunberg on Instagram and Twitter

@gretathunbergsweden on Facebook

STAY SAFE

Social media platforms can be a great way to stay in touch with your friends and follow your heroes – but always be sure to stay safe online. Always ask an adult before you go online, and never give away your full name, address, phone number, school or post photos of your location. If somebody leaves comments that make you feel uncomfortable, tell an adult.

GRETA THUNBERG:
A TIMELINE

Greta is born in Sweden, the daughter of an opera singer and actor.

January, 2003

Greta, age 15, skips school to protest outside the Swedish parliament for more action against climate change. She protests every day for three weeks.

August 20, 2018

More than 20,000 students in at least 270 cities take part in Friday school strikes. Greta is invited to speak at important climate talks across Europe.

December, 2018

February, 2019

Protests inspired by Greta take place in more than 30 countries, from Sweden to Brazil, India and the United States.

Time magazine features Greta as its cover star, hailing her as the voice of a generation.

May, 2019

September, 2019

Greta joins youth climate activists protesting outside the White House and speaks at the United Nations Climate Action Summit in New York to highlight the worrying lack of action to tackle climate change.

2011 — An eight-year-old Greta first learns of the climate crisis affecting our planet.

September, 2018 — Greta begins striking every Friday. Her 'Fridays for Future' movement calls on fellow pupils to protest climate issues by striking from their own schools.

January, 2019 — Greta travels for 32 hours by train to speak at the World Economic Forum in Davos, Switzerland. She tells industry leaders to act on climate change.

March, 2019 — Greta is nominated for a Nobel Peace Prize, as the number of pupils taking part in school strikes reaches more than 2 million people across 135 countries.

August, 2019 — Greta and her father set sail on a zero-carbon boat from Plymouth, UK, to New York. The journey takes two weeks.

December, 2019 — Greta is a guest speaker at the 25th Climate Change Summit in Santiago, Mexico.

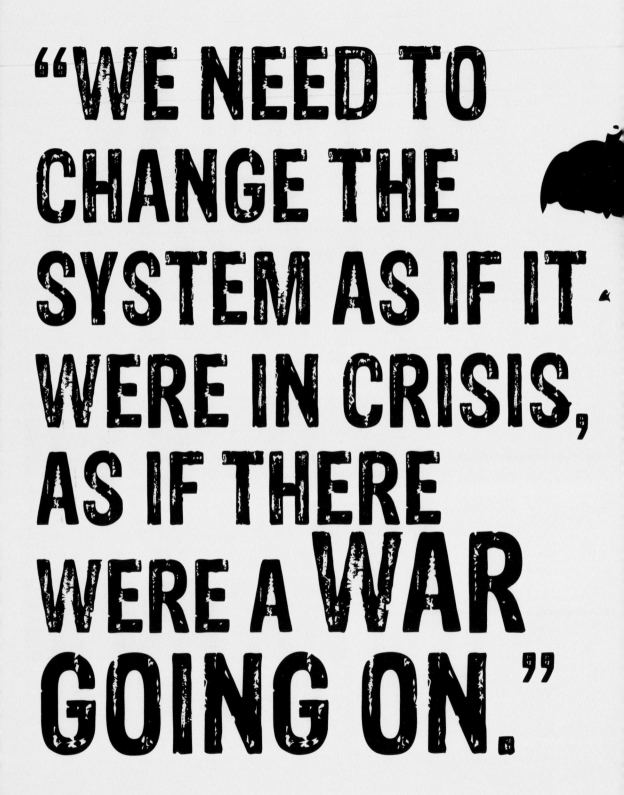

"WE NEED TO CHANGE THE SYSTEM AS IF IT WERE IN CRISIS, AS IF THERE WERE A WAR GOING ON."

GRETA'S INSPIRATIONS

Greta has been inspired by figures from history and the recent past to do the work she does. Seeing how others used their voices and actions to make a change helped to grow Greta's confidence, moving her to act on what is important to her.

ROSA PARKS

Greta has said that the first person to inspire her was American activist, Rosa Parks. "I learned she was an introvert, and I'm also an introvert," Greta says. Rosa demonstrated to Greta how **"one person can make such a huge difference"** – as Greta has gone on to inspire millions of people around the world to fight for action on climate change.

Rosa Parks was born in 1913 in the United States. Growing up in Montgomery, Alabama, she struggled to understand why black and white people were treated differently. On 1 December 1955, Rosa took a stand: she refused to give up her seat to a white person just because she was black. This small act transformed American society and led to a change in the law. Rosa continued to fight for equality and justice for everyone, whatever the colour of their skin. She remains a symbol of equality and freedom to many people today.

Rosa Parks

STUDENT RALLIES

Greta says her idea to strike from school was inspired by teen activists in the United States. When she read about these students, she realized that **children could create change.**

After a shooting at Marjory Stoneman Douglas High School in Parkland, Florida, in 2018, thousands of students across many states walked out of their lessons to take a stand against gun control. Multiple rallies followed, as well as the founding of a student-led movement called 'Never Again'.

The student protestors spoke clearly and thoughtfully about their cause, which made adults sit up and listen. In Florida, a bill was passed in response to their pleas. Though there are still many more battles being fought on the issue of gun control, this felt like a breakthrough, and it gave an **important voice to the younger generation.**

INSPIRING OTHERS

While Greta has been inspired by others, she has also become an inspiration in her own right. Her face is known worldwide as the unofficial poster girl for climate change, and people young and old have seen how **one person** can create a **ripple effect for change.**

LARGER THAN LIFE

In Bristol, UK, artist Jody Thomas painted a mural of Greta on an outdoor wall. It took over a week to paint this giant 15-metre-high portrait. Jody used water-based paints and limited his use of traditional spray paints as much as possible, to be kinder to the environment.

Jody wanted to honour Greta as a role model of our time and use his art to spread her powerful message. It's said that **a picture speaks a thousand words**, and here his picture expresses so much. Greta is shown in danger – among melting ice caps under a stormy sky. She is looking straight at the viewer, as though she is urging them to try to help before it is too late.

MAKING TRACKS

In 2019, Greta worked with pop rock band The 1975 to release a track, also called 'The 1975'. On the track, Greta speaks over a soft, instrumental background, reaching a whole new audience with her warnings about changes to our environment.

Through music, Greta emphasizes the science behind the climate crisis and the actions we need to take. She ends with a serious call to action:

"... WE CAN NO LONGER SAVE THE WORLD BY PLAYING BY THE RULES. BECAUSE THE RULES HAVE TO BE CHANGED. EVERYTHING NEEDS TO CHANGE. AND IT HAS TO START TODAY..."

ONE STEP AT A TIME

While Greta now confidently speaks before audiences of thousands of people at a time, she started out small. It was by persuading her family to make positive changes in their lives that Greta's confidence began to grow.

First, she convinced her family to stop eating meat and later to become vegan. She even convinced her international opera-singer mother to stop travelling by air – a huge feat since this affected her mother's job. When she could see that her family were making changes **because of her**, Greta felt listened to, and that felt good.

If you want to inspire others, try working up to a bigger audience by starting small, just like Greta did.

KEEP IT IN THE FAMILY

Speak to your family about your concerns, your reasons and the goals of your cause. Keep it factual and realistic so that they can get on board. Try to convince them to get involved, even if it's just in a small way. For example, they could help spread the word, or simply put up a poster at their school or workplace. Once your family is listening, you'll feel that other people are likely to do the same.

WHAT FRIENDS ARE FOR

Next, speak to your friends about your cause. Explain to them why it's important to you and what they can do to help. Once you have the support of just one friend or classmate, others are likely to follow.

BRANCHING OUT

When you feel confident that you have something to say and people are listening and interested, try thinking just a little bigger. Speak to teachers or get involved in local events. Act in a positive way so that others will want to follow your lead.

SPEAKING

OUT

Greta has spoken in front of the world's media, leading politicians and at climate rallies all over Europe and in the United States, addressing thousands of people at a time. But speaking in public does not come naturally to Greta, who admits to being very shy and only speaking when she has to.

When she was younger, Greta was diagnosed with selective mutism, a disorder that causes a person to become too distressed to speak in certain situations. Greta's parents were worried when their daughter agreed to speak in front of large audiences, but Greta bravely rose to the challenge.

"All my life I have been like the invisible girl at the back that no one sees or listens to."

If you'd like to share your passion in public and have something to say, try these tips to get you started:

START SMALL

The thought of speaking in front of a crowd may seem scary, so start by practising what you want to say in front of a friend or your family. Then slowly work your way up to a bigger crowd. Remember that the bigger the audience, the further you can spread your message.

HOLD YOUR NERVE

Remember that even global superstars can suffer from stage fright – it's completely normal. It means that what you want to say is important to you. So take some deep breaths and ask yourself what's the worst that can happen? Even if things don't go perfectly this time, you can try again in the future.

ASK FOR A REVIEW OF YOU

If you're keen to make yourself be heard, ask someone to give you feedback on what you're doing well and what you could be doing better. Perhaps you need to speak more slowly or just smile more? Every speaker needs feedback, to work out how to improve.

DESIGN A SIGN

Imagine you're joining a school strike – an eye-catching sign with a clever slogan will help to get your message across. Sketch out a design for a climate-strike sign on the next page or draw a poster to display at school.

TOP TIPS

Use contrasting colours for the words and background to make your message stand out.

Add pictures or symbols to illustrate your message.

Funny or serious slogans can work well. Work out what you want to say and keep it short.

Recycle thick cardboard or try using poster board.

Write in large bold letters that can be read from far away. Sketch them in pencil first.

Use materials that will survive bad weather – eco-friendly marker pens work well.

WRITE YOUR OWN
SPEECH

Greta plans her speeches carefully and writes them in advance. She researches her facts and checks them with experts to be sure they're correct. Greta asks her dad to read over her rough drafts. She makes sure that she is as prepared as she can be so that her words will have **the strongest impact possible.**

TOP TIPS

- Start by introducing yourself, and catch your audience's interest with a strong point. Tell them why you're there to talk to them.

- Make your speech hard to argue with. Give accurate facts, specific details and real examples.

- Break it down. Try writing three paragraphs, each focused on one main point of your argument.

- Use powerful adjectives. Greta said: "We are facing a disaster of **unspoken** sufferings for **enormous** amounts of people." Your speech should appeal to the emotions of your listeners.

- Use repetition to drive your point. Greta said: "You say nothing in life is black or white. But that is a lie. A very dangerous lie. Either we prevent 1.5 °C of warming or we don't. Either we avoid setting off that irreversible chain reaction beyond human control or we don't. Either we choose to go on as a civilization or we don't." **Make it memorable!**

Plan your own speech here.

Introduction: Introduce yourself. Why are you making this speech?

1st point:

2nd point:

3rd point:

Conclusion: What message do you want to leave with your listeners?

BONUS TIP: These ideas work just as well for writing a persuasive letter to your local MP.

CARE FOR THE PLANET, CARE FOR YOURSELF

Greta's work as a climate activist has, at times, left her feeling exhausted and overwhelmed. She has learned how important it is to care for herself, just as much as she cares for her cause. Try these techniques to keep yourself healthy so that you have enough **positive energy** to fight your fight.

Breathe. Take long deep breaths to calm your body and mind. Count to three as you breathe in, and again as you breathe out. Repeat for at least ten deep, calming breaths.

Meditate. Close your eyes and let your mind wander. Picture a place that makes you happy.

Put down your phone or tablet. Reducing your screen time will help clear your head and allow you to take in the world around you.

Go for a walk. Admire the simple beauty of nature. Notice the sights, sounds and smells. Explore woodland, the beach or somewhere you've never visited before.

Keep moving. Exercise not only keeps your body healthy, it also helps improve your mood. Dance, play a sport, swim, cycle – even just run around with friends!

Have other interests. Balance your interest in your cause alongside some hobbies. Take some time out to try drama, singing, writing, art, sports, cookery ... whatever makes you happy!

Keep a journal. Let your thoughts flow by writing them down. A journal can remind you of great ideas later on and prevent thoughts getting stuck swirling around in your head.

Ignore the haters. Greta knows that if people are criticizing her and her ideas, it's because they're threatened by her. So she must be making an impact!

Sleep. Don't forget to sleep! A good night's rest is one of the best things you can do to keep up your energy levels.

VOICE
OF A
GENERATION

Greta's words and actions have inspired
thousands of young people around the world
to join the fight against climate change, but
how much do you really know about her?
Take this quiz to see how big a fan of the
inspirational school striker you are.

1. **How old was Greta when she organized her first school strike?**

A. 13 ☐   B. 15 ☐   C. 16 ☐

2. **When is her birthday?**

A. 3 January ☐   B. 13 January ☐   C. 1 February ☐

3. **What is her sister's name?**

A. Beata ☐   B. Maja ☐   C. Elsa ☐

4. **Which band featured Greta's speeches on one of their singles?**

A. Foals ☐   B. The 1975 ☐   C. Friendly Fires ☐

5. Greta is...

A. Vegetarian ☐   B. Pescatarian ☐   C. Vegan ☐

6. How does she travel to her local school strikes?

A. Train ☐   B. Car ☐   C. Bicycle ☐

7. How many people follow Greta on Instagram?

A. 2 million+ ☐   B. 5 million+ ☐   C. 7 million+ ☐

8. What type of animal does Greta have as a pet?

A. Dog ☐   B. Cat ☐   C. Horse ☐

9. What job does her mother have?

A. Politician ☐   B. Opera singer ☐   C. Teacher ☐

10. How did Greta cross the Atlantic from the UK to New York in summer 2019?

A. Aeroplane ☐

B. Carbon-neutral boat ☐

C. Cruise ship ☐

You've taken the quiz, now check your answers below and add up how many you got right to reveal your score.

0–3
You've learned a little about Greta and her mission to raise the issue of climate change, but you could follow her work more closely.

4–7
You keep up to date with all the news about Greta and act on the important advice she gives.

8–10
You are totally in tune with Greta and her environmental messages, keep believing in her and remember, you are never too young to make a difference.

Answers: 1 – B, 2 –A, 3 –A, 4 – B, 5 – C, 6 – C, 7 – C, 8 –A, 9 – B, 10 – B.

CHANGE IS COMING

We know that our climate is changing, but not everyone realizes how it is already affecting us and how life on Earth may change for ever. Arming yourself with the facts and sharing them with your friends and family can help people to understand why it is so important to look after our planet.

DID YOU KNOW?

By 2050, 10 per cent of the world's population will be forced to leave their homes as sea levels rise and crops fail.

200 species become extinct every day – that's between 1,000 and 10,000 times the natural rate.

If pollution and over-fishing continue at their current rates, by 2048 there will be no fish left in our oceans.

Every day, about eight million pieces of plastic pollution find their way into our oceans. That's like dumping a rubbish truck full of plastic into our oceans every single minute.

The number of floods has doubled since 2004, while extreme temperatures, droughts and wildfires have more than doubled in the last 40 years.

The world's tropical forests are shrinking at an astonishing rate: the same as 30 football pitches every minute. Tropical deforestation is now responsible for 11 per cent of the world's CO_2 emissions.

Humans are using the Earth's resources faster than ever before – 1.75 times faster than the planet can regenerate them.

YOUR PLANET NEEDS YOU!

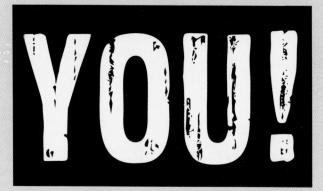

Greta cares deeply about communicating the crisis that is facing our climate across the world. The increase of the Earth's temperature is serious and affects humans, animals and plants, but if we all play our part in helping to protect the environment we can bring about real change.

"No one is too small to make a difference."

Here are 50 practical ways that you and your family and friends can help make a difference, from getting drastic on plastic to joining the fight against fast fashion.

50

Ditch **plastic bags** when shopping for groceries or other items. When you think that a single plastic bag can take up to 1,000 years to degrade, a **reusable bag** is the smart option. Just remember to wash it regularly!

49

Look for products that aren't packaged in **extra plastic** – fruit and veg such as bananas, apples and carrots don't need wasteful plastic wrappers. Look out for black plastic trays used to package meat, fruit and veggies – they are often non-recyclable.

48

Say no to straws… Many restaurants and take-away outlets are removing **plastic straws**, which are one of the most common plastic items found during beach cleans. Think twice about asking for a paper straw too, they are **rarely recycled**.

47

Chewing gum and bubble gum used to be made from a natural tree sap. These days, though, gum is more likely to be made from a polymer (plastic) that can take 500 years to decompose. Reach for a natural mint instead.

46

Wave goodbye to **wet wipes**. They may look like paper, but most contain plastic. They should not be flushed away like normal toilet paper – ones that are block sewers and waterways causing millions of pounds worth of damage and can find their way into our oceans.

45

Wrap snacks or cover food with **beeswax wraps** instead of clingfilm or foil. The natural wraps can be washed and reused time and again before being composted when they reach the end of their lives.

A WORLD OF PLASTIC IS NOT FANTASTIC

TIME TO CHANGE

RESPECT

44

B.Y.O. Planning on a hot chocolate or smoothie treat in town? Bring your own **reusable cup** for maximum enjoyment! Carrying your own reusable water bottle will cut your plastic use, too, and save you money. Look out for free refill stations to keep yourself refreshed.

43

Ban plastics from your bathroom — buy **soap and shampoo in bars.** Liquid soap needs five times more energy to produce and can use 20 times more packaging. **Bamboo toothbrushes** and biodegradable cotton buds are great swaps for traditional single-use plastic ones, too.

42

Microbeads are tiny pieces of plastic found in cosmetics and cleaning products. They have a huge impact on the environment, as they don't dissolve like other ingredients and can find their way into our oceans and the stomachs of fish and other marine mammals. Countries such as the UK and Sweden have banned the use of microbeads in cosmetics and cleaning products. Avoid ingredients such as polyethylene and polypropylene when choosing cosmetics.

41

Did you know that most disposable razors and sanitary products are packed with plastic that can end up in landfill, or worse still, in our waterways? When you grow up, you might start to use these products – always try to choose **reusable** versions, instead of disposable razors or sanitary products that are discarded after a single use. Remember that sanitary items should **never** be flushed down the toilet.

WHAT TO EAT

As the world's population grows every day – over 7.7 billion citizens share our planet – so does the demand to produce enough food for everyone to eat. Here are some ideas to help you and your family eat well without leaving a bad taste in your mouth.

40

Talk to your family about buying only what you need. About one third of all food produced for human consumption across the globe is wasted or lost, that's about 1.3 billion tonnes every year. This food has taken land, fresh water, labour, transport and refrigeration to produce. We can all play our part in helping to reduce food waste – here's how:

- Use shopping lists
- Love your leftovers
- Check and understand best before and use by dates
- Make the freezer your friend
- Compost your scraps

Eat less meat. After learning about how the food we eat can have a big effect on the planet, Greta decided to go **vegan**. She even persuaded her family to give up meat and dairy too. Meat, particularly red meat, takes more energy to produce (think of the food, water and land a single cow needs during its lifetime). Animals also produce a lot of waste, including methane gas, a damaging greenhouse gas. Coud your family try a day or two without eating meat each week? Even a few meat-free meals will have a positive environmental effect.

The saying 'there's plenty more fish in the sea' is sadly no longer true. Our appetite for fish and seafood and methods of catching fish have caused fish stocks in the oceans to fall at an incredible rate. Governments are closely monitoring the fishing industry and banning illegal fishing of endangered fish. You can help, too, by choosing **sustainable species** of fish to eat instead of endangered ones. Switch out Atlantic salmon or bluefin tuna for yummy pollock fish fingers or enjoy a sustainable haddock fish supper.

37

Think local. The fewer miles that food has had to travel to reach you, the smaller its carbon footprint is likely to be. Tips to help reduce the environmental impact when buying food include: **shopping locally** (leaving the car at home, where possible) and eating food that's in season.

36

Opt for **organic produce** where possible and affordable. It may cost a little more, but it's better for our bodies, as it reduces our exposure to **toxic pesticides.** Animals reared to produce organic meat and dairy products enjoy the highest standards of animal welfare and are not given antibiotics and other drugs unless needed, while fruit and veg are grown without using unnatural pesticides and fertilizers.

35

Up to 40 per cent of a farmer's crop can go to waste because supermarkets demand that fruit and veg come in certain shapes and sizes. Check out the wonderfully **'wonky'** section in your supermarket – a misshapen carrot or an ugly cauliflower is just as nutritious and tasty, while helping to **tackle food waste**.

34

Give G.I.Y. a go! Discover how green your fingers are by **growing it yourself**. Sowing salad or veggies at home is easier and cheaper than you may think and the good news is that you don't even need a garden to get started: a small space such as a balcony or a windowsill can work well too. Try carrots, beans or herbs, which will taste great and **reduce your carbon footprint**.

33

Buying **fairtrade** products can help make sure a farmer is paid a fair wage. This means that they can cover their costs, earn enough money to have a decent standard of living and invest in their farms to keep their crops healthy, without needing to use cheap fertilizers, which can harm the environment.

32

Palm oil is a vegetable oil that comes from palm trees and is used in a whole range of products, from doughnuts to detergents, shampoo to sweets. Many of the trees used to make palm oil grow in areas of tropical rainforest. The trees are cut down to produce the oil or burned to clear areas to grow new trees. This process, known as **deforestation**, destroys the places where plants and wildlife live, including the habitats of endangered species such as the orang-utan and Sumatran rhino. Look for products that contain sustainable palm oil when shopping.

31

Be friendly to bees! Brilliant bees pollinate many of our food crops, from cherries to coffee plants, tomatoes to turnips, yet many bee species face extinction across the globe. Try planting some wildflowers, building a bee hotel and avoiding pesticides in your garden or at school.

WAY TO GO

The transport sector is the fastest-growing contributor to climate emissions. Every car journey or flight we take is adding greenhouse gases into the atmosphere – a frightening thought.

Air travel is responsible for about 5 per cent of human-caused global warming. It affects the climate through the greenhouse gases released as aeroplanes burn fuel, and through the heat-trapping effect of the condensation formed by the contrail clouds an aircraft leaves in the sky.

Greta discovered these facts at a time when her mother was performing in opera concerts all over the world, travelling to far-flung destinations by plane. Greta decided that she herself would no longer travel anywhere by air, accepting there were some countries she would most likely never see. But for Greta, it was an easy decision. She then shared facts on the environmental impact her mother's travel was having with her family, which persuaded them to give up flying too.

On Greta's advice, Malena Ernman travelled abroad less, the family made any long journeys by rail and bought an electric car (to be used only when absolutely necessary). For everyday travel, they rode their bikes. Greta had used her voice to influence her family to make positive changes – a skill that would go on to serve her well.

Turn the page to continue the countdown and find ways that you and your family can reduce your carbon footprint when you travel.

30

Being climate conscious is often not the cheapest option and not everyone can afford an electric car. But you can take steps to reduce your carbon footprint by thinking about the short car journeys you make – are there times when you could **walk or cycle** to school, activities or the shops instead of driving?

29

If your journey is just a little too far to cycle or walk, try using **public transport** instead of a car. Find a local bus, train, tram, metro or underground train going in your direction. Public transport can cut down carbon emissions hugely: for example, by 37 million tons per year in the United States!

28

Look for **eco-friendly** public transport. Many cities are investing in new transport systems that are built with the environment in mind. Some use solar power or hybrid engines. If your city or town doesn't have these options, consider writing to your local council to ask for them.

27

Plan ahead! Most public transport systems have apps you can use to plan your route. Check the apps in advance to find which buses or trains you need to take and where to find them. By planning ahead, you can reduce the number of journeys you take – and feel confident about your travel by public transport too.

26

If you do have to travel by car, arrange to **travel in a group**, with people who are travelling to the same place as you. Cities in some countries provide special car-sharing lanes for cars with two or more people inside – meaning that you can actually get where you want faster, bypassing the rest of the traffic!

25

Still on the subject of cars, remind the driver to **switch off the engine** when the car is stationary. You don't need the engine running when you're in a traffic jam or have stopped to drop someone off. Turning off the engine will reduce the pollution your car emits into the air.

In April 2019, Greta made headlines when she spent two days travelling from Rome to London by **train** to address the UK parliament. Greta and her father saved an estimated 400 kg of carbon each by not flying. Could train travel make you an **eco hero**?

23

Then, in August 2019, Greta made headlines again when she and her father travelled across the Atlantic Ocean for 15 days on board an **emission-free yacht.** The yacht, built for racing, was fitted with solar panels and underwater turbines to generate zero-carbon emissions. While Greta doesn't expect everyone to travel by boat, she encourages people to find low-carbon transport **alternatives** wherever possible.

22

If you do need to travel by air, **choose direct flights** instead of flights that stop in other cities along the way. As take-off and landing use the most fuel, reducing the amount of times you start and stop will in turn reduce your carbon footprint.

21

Another way to reduce your environmental impact if you need to use air travel is to **pack lightly**. An aeroplane uses more fuel the heavier it is, so the fewer bags it has to carry, the lower its carbon footprint will be. Leave that extra pair of shoes at home!

SET THE
TREND

The fashion industry has a devastating impact on the environment. Did you know that after the oil industry, it's one of the next largest polluters in the world? The good news is that there are plenty of practical things we can do to help, by shopping in a sustainable way and encouraging others to do the same.

20

Cheap clothing or **fast fashion** means that we buy and throw away more clothes and textiles than ever before. Only around 15 per cent is donated or recycled, with the rest going directly to landfill or to be incinerated. Think twice about whether you really need to buy an item, and swap or recycle anything you no longer love.

19

Like it or not, we live in a throwaway society. Many people are too quick to get rid of an item, even if it only has a small hole or fraying seam. If we **mend our clothes**, we can mend our ways, meaning less waste in landfill. Many repairs can be made without a machine, so give sewing a go!

18

While you're about it, why not give old clothes and accessories a new lease of life with **DIY design**? Sew on decorations, get out your scissors to change a garment's shape or draw on patterns and slogans with fabric pens. Giving old clothes a makeover reduces waste, reduces the need for new ones and lets your creativity shine.

If you do need to buy clothes, try shopping at **vintage** or **second-hand charity** shops. You might be surprised at the amazing treasures you can find! You'll save these items from going to waste, and you'll reduce your carbon footprint by avoiding new clothes that take energy to make. Don't forget that you can donate old clothes to these shops too.

16

Another way to get a whole new look without having an impact on the environment is to have a **clothing swap**. Ask friends and siblings to find and share clothes they no longer wear or that no longer fit. The perfect outfit may be closer than you think!

15

The regular use of chemicals to dye or bleach our clothes causes big problems for the environment. Look for **organic fibres** that require fewer chemical fertilizers and pesticides and less water to grow. While sustainable brands may come with a higher price tag than fast fashion, the clothes you wear will be kinder to the planet.

14

Look at the fabrics of the clothes you're buying. Choose **eco-friendly** materials such as organic cotton, bamboo and hemp. These require less energy and water to produce. Some clothes are even made of recycled plastics, saving the plastic from ending up in landfill or our oceans.

13

Speaking of materials, follow Greta's lead and switch out any clothing or accessories made of animal products. These include wool, leather and fur. Farming the animals specifically to make these products pollutes both the air and water. Look out for clothes made of a **plant-based** or **renewable fabric alternative**.

12

Many of our clothes are produced in countries such as China, Bangladesh and India, whose factories rely on energy produced by burning coal – the dirtiest type of energy in terms of carbon emissions. Check labels on clothes and choose outfits that are made in countries powered by more **renewable energy**.

11

Give your washing machine a break! Every time we wash a synthetic garment, about 1,900 individual microfibres are released into the water, making their way into our oceans. The fibres are swallowed by tiny aquatic organisms, which are then eaten by small fish and later by bigger fish – introducing plastic into our food chain. So if your clothes look (and smell) clean, **wear them again**.

BE A HERO AT HOME

Did you know that you can be an eco hero without even leaving your house? Here are ten top tips to save your household energy and water (plus money) and lead a greener lifestyle every day. Share these facts with friends and family to save even more of the Earth's precious resources from being wasted. Not all super heroes wear a cape!

10

Take a **quick shower** instead of a long bath. It might take 80 litres of hot water to fill the bathtub, compared to only about 35 litres for a short shower. If you have a power shower, think about installing an eco shower-head to save water. Take the challenge: can you shower in three minutes or under?

9

Turn off the tap when cleaning your teeth to save six litres of water per minute. Brushing twice a day, two minutes at a time, seven days a week means the wasted water quickly adds up if you leave the tap running. Check for water leaks or dripping taps around the home. A dripping tap can waste 15 litres of water a day, or 5,500 litres of water a year, while a leaky toilet can use up an extra five bathtubs worth of water. **What a waste!**

8

Could your family's tablets or smartphones be repaired to add extra years to their life cycles? Taking care of your devices will make them last longer and create less waste. Decide whether you really need the latest model of a games console or tablet and remember to **recycle** any broken devices.

Ask whoever pays your energy bills at home to see whether you are already using a **green energy supplier**, or whether it's possible to switch to one. It could be cheaper and the green energy you use would reduce the negative impact on the environment by producing a smaller carbon footprint.

Going Green

Green energy is energy we get from renewable sources, rather than non-renewable sources like oil or coal.

The renewable sources used to make green energy include:

- **wind power** – usually generated by wind turbines
- **solar power** – produced when sunlight is absorbed by solar panels and converted into power
- **hydroelectric power** – where large volumes of flowing water turn a turbine, producing energy
- **wave power** – captured from waves in our oceans, rivers, lakes and canals
- **tidal power** – where energy is produced as the tide changes, which happens as a result of the moon's gravitational pull
- **biofuels** – when biological materials, such as plant matter, are used as a fuel sources
- **geothermal power** – uses heat from under the Earth's surface to heat homes and other buildings.

6

Buy **low-energy lightbulbs**, such as LED bulbs — they use a fraction of the energy needed to light an incandescent bulb and could last ten times longer. Turn off lights when they're not needed, too.

5

Switched-on people know to **switch off gadgets** when not in use. Computers, TVs, printers and phone chargers all use energy in standby mode that could easily be saved. Encourage friends and family to turn off electronic devices when they're not being used.

4

Feeling cold? **Grab a jumper** before turning up the central heating. The same goes for warm weather — strip off a layer before opting for air-conditioning (if you have it) to help save energy.

3

Drying clothes on a washing line outside or on an airer inside, instead of using a tumble dryer, could save every household **more than a ton of CO_2** a year. Your clothes will last longer and you'll save money on your energy bills, too. A no-brainer!

2

Only use the dishwasher or washing machine with a full load and drop eco-friendly detergents in the drawer. These are made from non-toxic and natural ingredients, rather than the **toxic chemicals** contained in modern cleaning products, which can pose risks to our health and end up in our waterways.

1

Streaming videos requires more energy than you might think, and rarely does that energy come from renewable sources. The data servers that bring us our favourite programmes and channels require a great deal of cooling, and are estimated to consume at least 1 per cent of the world's electricity every year, a figure that is expected to rise. **Cut down your screen time** to help reduce carbon emissions.

HOW BIG IS YOUR CARBON FOOTPRINT?

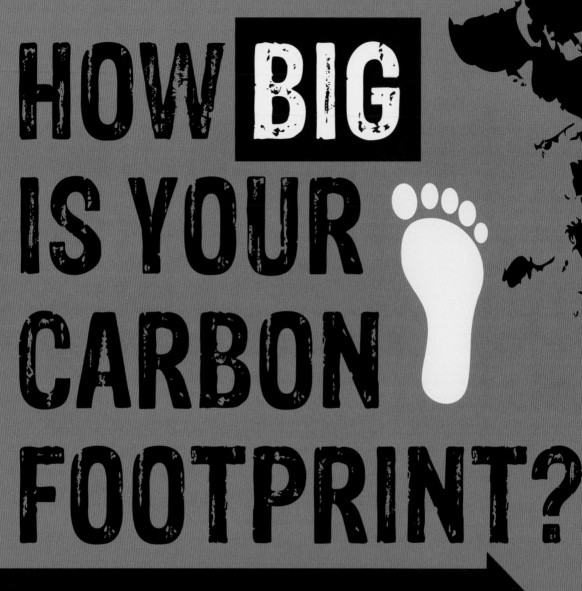

Greta has set us all a target to reduce our carbon footprint, in order to slow down global warming. This involves governments and big companies committing to change, but individuals can make a difference, too. Every little thing adds up! Take this quiz to find out your impact on the world.

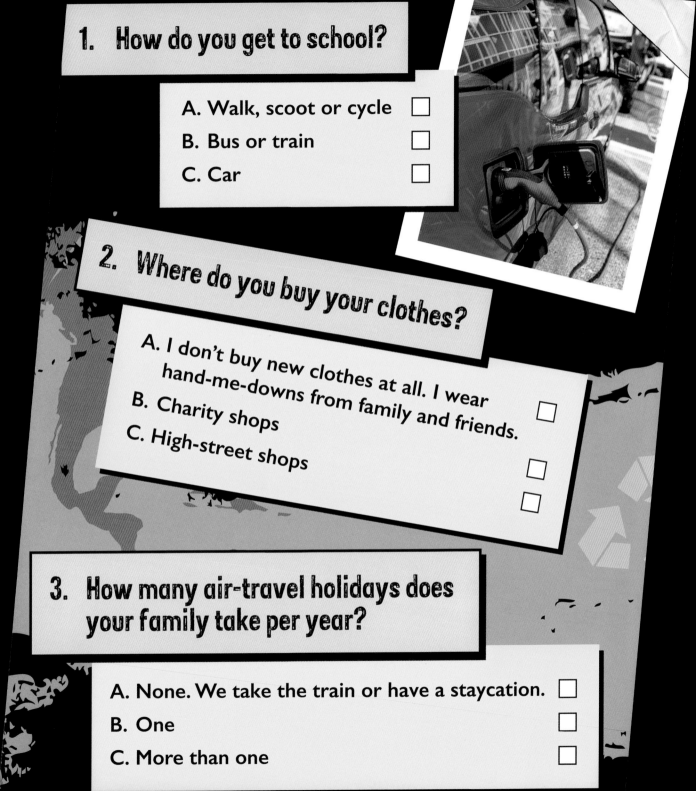

1. How do you get to school?

A. Walk, scoot or cycle ☐
B. Bus or train ☐
C. Car ☐

2. Where do you buy your clothes?

A. I don't buy new clothes at all. I wear hand-me-downs from family and friends. ☐
B. Charity shops ☐
C. High-street shops ☐

3. How many air-travel holidays does your family take per year?

A. None. We take the train or have a staycation. ☐
B. One ☐
C. More than one ☐

4. How often do you eat meat?

A. Not at all. ☐
B. 1–3 times per week. ☐
C. More than three times per week. ☐

5. Do you turn off lights, appliances and switches when you're not using them?

A. Always! ☐
B. Most of the time… ☐
C. I usually forget. ☐

6. Which products do you have in your bathroom?

A. Bamboo toothbrush, bar soap, bar shampoo. ☐
B. Bar of soap, but plastic bottles of shampoo and conditioner. ☐
C. Liquid soap and bottles upon bottles of cosmetic products! ☐

7. Does your family recycle and compost?

A. Yes, always. ☐

B. Most of the time. ☐

C. Never – everything goes into a bin bag. ☐

8. When you go out, do you remember your water bottle and reusable bags?

A. Yes, I always carry them with me. ☐

B. Sometimes I forget to take my water bottle. ☐

C. No, I use disposable cups and new carrier bags each time. ☐

Now count up your answers to find out your results.

Mostly As

You are living like Greta! You are clearly conscious of your lifestyle choices and making a big effort to take care of our planet. Your carbon footprint is low.

Mostly Bs

You're on the right track! You are making sensible climate-friendly decisions but could work even harder to reduce your carbon footprint.

Mostly Cs

Your carbon footprint is high. Think about ways that you could reduce your emissions to help our planet. Share these ideas with family and friends.

"RIGHT HERE, RIGHT NOW IS WHERE WE DRAW THE LINE. THE WORLD IS WAKING UP. AND CHANGE IS COMING, WHETHER YOU LIKE IT OR NOT."

ARE YOU CLUED UP ON CLIMATE CHANGE?

Take this quiz to discover whether you're a climate champion, then share the facts with family and friends.

1. Global warming...

A. Causes sea levels to rise. ☐

B. Results in extreme weather events, such as heat waves or hurricanes. ☐

C. Threatens wildlife all over the world with extinction. ☐

D. All of the above. ☐

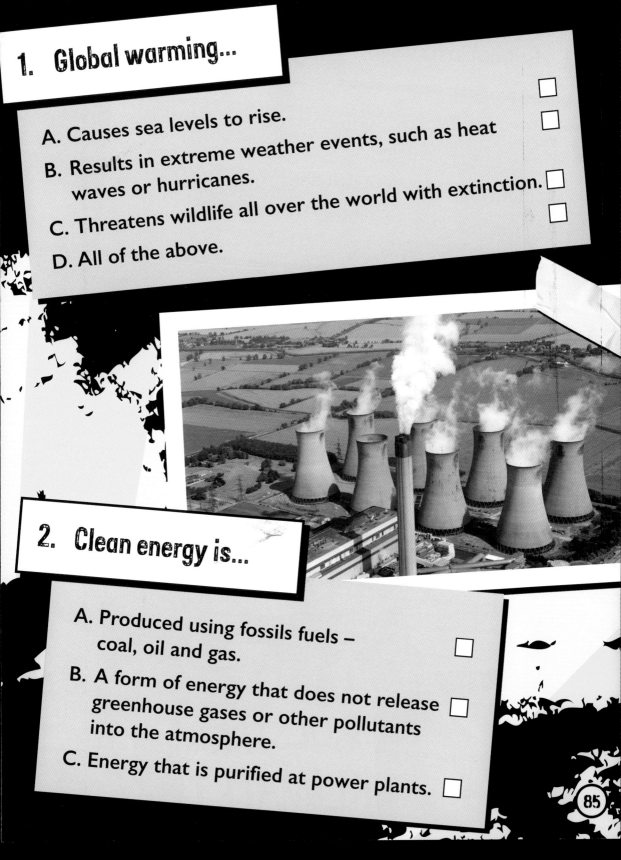

2. Clean energy is...

A. Produced using fossils fuels – coal, oil and gas. ☐

B. A form of energy that does not release greenhouse gases or other pollutants into the atmosphere. ☐

C. Energy that is purified at power plants. ☐

3. School strikes...

A. Raise awareness of important issues such ☐
   as climate change.

B. Only take place in Sweden. ☐

C. Are not taken seriously by politicians. ☐

4. Greenhouse gases are...

A. Gases in the Earth's atmosphere that trap heat. They include carbon dioxide and methane. ☐

B. Gases that do not cause harm to the environment. ☐

C. Gases that are produced in greenhouses. ☐

5. A greenhouse gas released from landfill sites is called...

A. Carbon dioxide ☐

B. Methane ☐

C. Water vapour ☐

6. A plastic bag takes how long to fully degrade?

A. Up to one year ☐

B. Up to 100 years ☐

C. Up to 1,000 years ☐

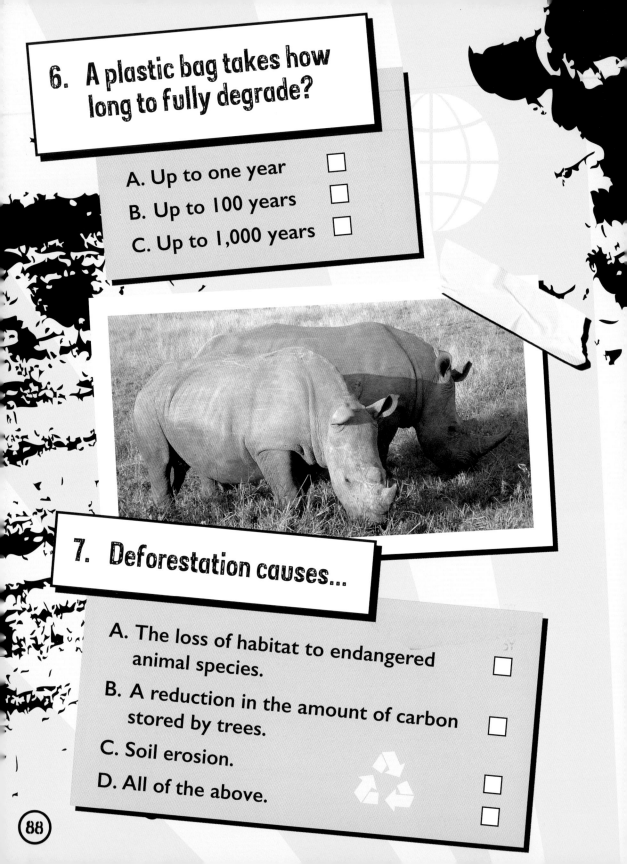

7. Deforestation causes...

A. The loss of habitat to endangered animal species. ☐

B. A reduction in the amount of carbon stored by trees. ☐

C. Soil erosion.

D. All of the above. ☐

☐

8. An easy way to reduce our carbon emissions is to...

A. Cut down on the amount of red meat we eat.

B. Avoid buying fast fashion.

C. Turn off gadgets around the home.

D. All of the above.

You've taken the quiz, now check your answers below and add up how many you got right to reveal your score.

0–3

It's time to brush up on the facts about climate change. Read up on the issues that are affecting our planet to help make a difference.

4–7

You're keen to be green and understand about global warming. Take the next steps to reduce your carbon footprint.

8–10

Just like Greta, you're passionate about learning about how to look after the environment. Now take action to become a true climate champion!

Answers: 1 – D, 2 – B, 3 – A, 4 – A, 5 – B, 6 – C, 7 – D, 8 – D.

89

BE THE CHANGE

Every person, every day, can change their habits to reduce their impact on the environment. Look back at some of the ideas in this book and make your own pledges to help save the planet – from spreading the important facts about climate change to saving energy in the home.

Start today!

Today I will...

_____

_____

_____

This week I will...

_____

_____

_____

This year I will...

_____

_____

_____

GLOSSARY

biodegradable: anything that can decompose or be broken down by microorganisms such as bacteria.

carbon dioxide (CO_2): a gas released by the burning of coal, gas, oil and wood that traps heat in the atmosphere.

carbon footprint: the amount of carbon dioxide one human releases into the environment in a year.

climate: the average pattern of weather conditions in an area over a long period of time.

deforestation: when humans clear or cut down forests, including rainforests, resulting in a loss of habitat for the plants and animals that live there.

environmental activist: a person who campaigns to bring about political change to protect the environment.

fossil fuels: coal, oil and gas, which are produced from the breakdown of ancient plants and animals over millions of years.

global warming: the increase in the Earth's average temperature over a long period of time.

greenhouse effect: the warming of the Earth's surface and the air above it, caused by gases in the air that trap energy from the sun.

greenhouse gases: gases in the Earth's atmosphere that trap heat. They include carbon dioxide, methane, ozone and nitrous oxide.

Nobel Peace Prize: a prestigious prize awarded to a person or group of people for their important work in the promotion of world peace.

microbeads: tiny pieces of plastic found in cosmetics or cleaning products that are not biodegradable.

renewable energy: energy that is produced without polluting the air or water, using natural resources such as wind, water and sunshine. It is also known as 'clean' or 'green' energy.

INDEX

PICTURE CREDITS

The publisher would like to thank the following sources for their kind permission to reproduce the pictures in this book.

Anders Hellberg: 16–17, 48

Bengt Nyman: 19r

European Parliament: 21

Freepik: 141

Getty Images: Cover – Axel Heimken/Contributor

Rhianne Hawkins: 29

Shutterstock.com:
9, 19l, 23l, 47, 55, 86–87 – Liv Oeian; 13 – Per Grunditz; 14-15r – FloridaStock; 23r, 64 – lev radin; 26 – neftali; 27 – David Tran Photo; 30 – Steve Vas/ Featureflash Photo Agency; 33 – FooTToo; 35 – Roland Marconi; 37r –Ink Drop; 51 – Mauro Ujetto; 56 – Split Second Stock; 58 – Thinglass; 66–67 – leungchopan; 68 – Rishiken; 71 – PNK Photo; 72 – mervas; 75 – GaudiLab; 76 – Africa Studio; 85 – Neil Mitchell.

Unsplash: 6l – American Public Power Association; 6r, 36–37l, 37c – Markus Spikse; 7l – John Cameron; 7r – Zbynek Burival; 52 neonbrand; 79 John Cameron; 90 Bob Blob